The Real Life Fugitive

Sam Sheppard and the Original Trial of the Century

ABSOLUTE CRIME

By Wallace Edwards

Absolute Crime Books

www.absolutecrime.com

© 2013. All Rights Reserved.

Cover Image © lbtn - Fotolia.com

Table of Contents

ABOUT US 3

INTRODUCTION 5

CHAPTER 1: THE EARLY DAYS 14

CHAPTER 2: MURDER IN THE SUBURBS 23

CHAPTER 3: THE INVESTIGATION 37

CHAPTER 4: THE TRIAL OF THE CENTURY 54

CHAPTER 5: PRISON LIFE 71

CHAPTER 6: THE SECOND TRIAL 94

CHAPTER 7: LATER LIFE 99

CHAPTER 8: LEGACY 105

CONCLUSION 109

BIBLIOGRAPHY 112

About Us

Absolute Crime publishes only the best true crime literature. Our focus is on the crimes that you've probably never heard of, but you are fascinated to read more about. With each engaging and gripping story, we try to let readers relive moments in history that some people have tried to forget.

Remember, our books are not meant for the faint at heart. We don't hold back—if a crime is bloody, we let the words splatter across the page so you can experience the crime in the most horrifying way!

If you enjoy this book, please visit our homepage to see other books we offer; if you have any feedback, we'd love to hear from you!

Introduction

Moonlight shone across Lake Erie as Dr. Sheppard and his wife, Marilyn, jumped from their motorboat into the cool, dark water. Waterskiing after midnight sounded like a refreshing way to end the mid-summer evening by their lakeside home in Bay Village, Ohio.

The heat of the day had dissipated, and the sun's fiery orb had long since melted into the horizon, gearing up for a beautiful Fourth of July weekend. A warm breeze rippled the water, water that sometimes churned up violent waves without warning, while at other times stilling into a shimmering sheet of glass.

A friend and neighbor sat at the controls, waiting for the couple to slip on their skis and give him the go-ahead. Dr. Sheppard, or Dr. Sam as most people called him, got his skis on first, but he didn't have to wait long for his athletic wife.

"Okay, I'm ready," Marilyn called to him, treading water a few feet away. He wasted no time waving his arm in a wide arc, signaling to the driver.

The couple could hear the duel outboards rev and could feel the power pulling them through the water, slowly at first and then faster and faster. They gripped their tow bars, bending at the knees, letting the speed bring them to the surface until they were both upright, skiing side-by-side across the deserted lake.

Marilyn wore a modest one-piece bathing suit that flattered her slender figure. Thirty-one years old and four months along in her second pregnancy, she still looked as fit as the day she'd graduated from high school. She had her thick brunette hair tucked up in a white bathing cap, customary for women of the 1950s. Balancing easily behind the aluminum boat, she enjoyed the freedom of waterskiing and the spray of the water splashing against her bare skin.

The houses along the shore blurred past them as the couple flew around the lake with abandon. They couldn't help smiling in the fast-moving shadows, thrilled as the boat pulled them into the darkness. Pretty soon the houselights dimmed behind them as they flew further and further from shore—in a lake so enormous that Marilyn sometimes felt as if she could get lost at sea forever. She glanced at her husband, skiing expertly alongside her, and felt reassured. Still, anything could happen at that speed, at that hour, where the watery darkness obscured visibility, making it impossible to see what was waiting ahead—and what waited ahead was a brutal and bloody murder. Marilyn Sheppard had only a few days left to live.

On July 3, 1954, Marilyn woke to the sound of water lapping against the shore beneath her open, upper-story bedroom window. A semi-private beach stretched out below the bluff upon which their house stood, and the soothing sound of waves rose like music through the mature maple trees that shaded their white, cape-cod-style home. A burst of light reached in the dormer window through a partially upraised shade, as the sun rose lazily, spreading itself over the suburban rooftops in the upscale neighborhood.

Marilyn tilted her head and listened for her seven-year-old son, Chip, who lay in the next room, but she didn't hear anything. *He's still sleeping*, she decided, remembering that he'd stayed up late the night before. They named him Sam after his father but called him Chip so as not to get the two mixed up.

Next, she listened for any sign of their houseguest, Dr. Lester Hoversten, an associate of Sam's from medical school. Hoversten had recently taken up residence in their master bedroom, since Marilyn preferred the guest room during the summer months, because it faced the lake. Hoversten, a night owl, usually slept until noon, which was just as well. The man gave Marilyn the creeps. Sometimes it felt as if Sam put Lester's needs above hers. Sure, Lester could use a place to stay while he looked for work, but he didn't have to leave his clothes lying around, and he could have better manners over all. *No wonder his wife kicked him out*, she mused, *not to mention the hospital that recently fired him*. She resented his presence, and he knew it. She also resented a past sexual innuendo he'd thrown her way. "Thank goodness he's staying elsewhere tonight," she said under her breath as she pushed the white bedspread aside. She and Sam had invited their neighbors, the Aherns, over for dinner, and she looked forward to Lester leaving.

She slid her legs over the edge of the bed and contemplated the long day ahead. She should be waking eagerly on a holiday weekend but felt a bit overwhelmed. She had a lot to do to prepare for the Fourth of July. Sam had volunteered to entertain a large group of interns and their significant others at a cookout the following day. He hadn't discussed it with her before offering to host the event. Didn't she have any say in the matter? She was pregnant after all, had he forgotten? Her husband had brushed her mood off, and didn't understand why she had blown things out of proportion.

Earlier that morning, Dr. Sam had slipped quietly through the kitchen and stepped into the garage where he'd parked his Lincoln the previous evening. His medical profession provided the best of everything: a dream house with a money view, a Lincoln, a Jaguar, a boathouse, and the thirteen-foot motorboat he'd purchased with the Houks, who lived a few doors down.

After backing out of the driveway, he drove a mere mile down the road to Bay Village Hospital, a mid-nineteenth-century stone mansion now owned by the Sheppard clan. The hospital had a pitched roof of fish-scale tile and numerous gables rising along its upper stories. Turrets, with conical spires, reached nobly to the sky only outdone in height by numerous brick chimneys. Three stories below, a row of Roman arches stood like sentinels atop the stone steps. The place exuded wealth, and so did the Sheppards.

Sam and his brothers, Drs. Steve and Richard, as well as their father, worked at Bay Village, having built it into a thriving practice. Even on a holiday weekend, the three brothers—all osteopathic physicians like their dad—attended to patients well into the afternoon. Recently, the foursome had posed for a picture, had stood there, father and sons, feeling as if they were on the top of the world. Little did they know that tragedy would soon strike, and all their hard work and success—even their reputations—would flounder like a four-masted ship in a storm.

Chapter 1: The Early Days

Sam Sheppard had grown up in a nurturing environment and had become accustomed to things going his way. During his privileged youth, he excelled at everything he did, especially turning out for sports. His athletic prowess gained him popularity and won him the attention of Marilyn Reese, who attended the same junior high school, one grade ahead.

Marilyn, equally athletic and attractive, managed an introduction via another student in the gymnasium while Sam dribbled a basketball. A spark ignited between the two inexperienced sweethearts, and she and Sam started passing notes back and forth during recess, flirting and stepping knee-deep into their first serious crush.

Throughout high school, Sam scored star positions in every sport in which he participated, even competing at the state level during track season. His peers elected him class president during his last three years of school and voted him most likely to succeed.

Marilyn had her own skills and actively took part in many clubs, such as the Dance Club and the Booster Club, but no one, including Marilyn, could compete with Sam Sheppard.

When she reached the twelfth grade, she asked him to a barn dance, which he happily attended. After slow dancing and mingling with the other students, the couple stole away alone, strolling hand in hand under the Ohio moon. At one point they stopped to share an innocent kiss. Being a year older, Marilyn had no qualms about expressing her feelings. "I love you," she whispered, leaning in a little closer. Sam smiled boyishly and said that he felt the same. That sealed the deal and they became an official twosome.

They were a popular pair, destined to be married, often seen side-by-side, smiling and holding hands. A bright future awaited this smart, attractive young couple of the upper crust.

After graduating from high school, Marilyn attended Skidmore College for one year. She planned to earn a liberal arts degree but would have preferred to major in everything Sam Sheppard. She daydreamed about him and couldn't get used to not seeing him on a regular basis; even daily letters couldn't take the place of her dream boy. Sam may have preferred more of a challenge, but he knew how lucky he was to have a young lady such as Marilyn vying for his attention—and if she didn't get it, she let him know how blue she felt. Her lack of academic focus resulted in poor grades, and she didn't bother enrolling for her sophomore year.

Around the time Marilyn dropped out of college, Sam enrolled in Hanover, a private liberal arts college in Indiana and the alma mater of his father and brothers. He vacillated between wanting to get married to Marilyn and wanting to date other women. He took a couple other women out, but Marilyn became extremely depressed, so he abandoned the idea.

After Hanover, Sam attended medical school in Southern California, where he eventually sent for Marilyn. She was an asset, helping Sam focus on his studies and helping him study for exams. In the couple's spare time they stayed active, making the most of the sun and the outdoors.

One day they might ride bikes or go to the beach. The next, they might take a walk or play a game of tennis. For a couple's match one afternoon, Marilyn dressed in a striped short-sleeved shirt, Keds, bobbysocks and white shorts. Her left ring finger proudly displayed a new ring.

Blessed with youth and vitality, the couple worked to stay at the peak of fitness and made tennis look easy. After playing a few rounds, Sam pulled his t-shirt off and tossed it courtside, so he could soak up the sun in only shorts and tennis shoes. Marilyn admired his physique and his stature. He walked over to her and they posed for a photograph, side-by-side, as usual. She reached her right arm around his waist, and he wrapped his left arm around her shoulders. They held their rackets to their sides and smiled at their friends on the other side of the camera.

Marilyn had pretty, ruby-red lips and a Mona-Lisa smile. At nineteen she stood next to her sweetheart for another picture. She never dressed provocatively and always looked well put together. Very much a lady of the fifties, she wore a knee-length, light-colored dress with short sleeves, white bobbysocks and brown penny loafers. She kept her chin-length hair off her forehead and face, with her bangs in a tight roll. Sam stood to her left in saddle shoes, a lightweight tan jacket over a dark shirt that was tucked into his tan trousers. She held her hands loosely in front of her; he held his behind his back. Twelve years from that date, her shiny brunette hair would be matted with blood. Her smiling face would be unrecognizable, and Sam, the love of her life, would be the prime suspect in her brutal murder.

# # #

In 1945, no one could have foreseen the nightmare awaiting them. But at the time, there was much to look forward to. Sam continued his studies in California and formally asked Marilyn to marry him. They had an intimate ceremony a week after Valentine's Day. She had a swath of white flowers in her hair and hope in her heart. But time afforded no honeymoon, which disappointed the new bride. Medical school came first. Marilyn worked part time and took care of their small apartment, looking forward to the time when her husband would be a doctor.

Before long, Marilyn conceived their first child. While the baby grew in her belly, lust grew in her husband's heart, and he started fooling around with other women, a habit he would continue for the next several years. Marilyn gave birth to their son and often waited at home alone caring for the baby, resenting her absent husband and feeling blue.

Sam became a doctor in 1948. He had an extremely demanding schedule, so all the domestic chores, including the childrearing, continued to fall on Marilyn. Two years later, while the young couple still lived in California, their marital problems came to a head when Sam started falling for a woman named Margaret Kauzor. He decided break the news to Marilyn, who became distraught. In the end, the affair didn't break up their marriage, but an atmosphere of distrust and resentment hung over the young family.

Chapter 2: Murder in the Suburbs

The prosperity of the 1950s ushered in the suburban boom, a perfect time for the Sheppards to move back to Ohio and purchase a waterfront home on Lake Erie. They would have been hard pressed to find a better place to raise their son Chip. From their deck they could watch the activity on the lake, such as sailboats gliding by, or enjoy the local waterfowl, like egrets, ducks and herons. In their yard, chipmunks scrambled up the tree trunks, delighting the neighborhood kids. Marilyn considered this move a brand new start.

She and her husband filled their new home with a modest amount of furniture, some bought on credit. Marilyn worked hard to keep the place tidy and loved to entertain small groups of friends. On occasion, they hired a window washer named Richard Eberling to give Marilyn a hand. She treated him well, sometimes chatting with him and offering him milk and cookies, or a lemonade on a hot summer's day. He got to know her and Chip and even their family dog, Koke. She didn't seem to notice, but he admired her long tan legs and how she looked in her short shorts and little summery tops. Marilyn, on the other hand, didn't pay any undo attention to him. She loved her husband even if he didn't have much time for his family.

In spite of the beautiful home he shared with his wife and son, Dr. Sheppard wasted no time getting wrapped up in another affair, this time with an attractive lab technician named Susan Hayes. They started having sex during the holiday season in 1952, after Susan began working at Bay View Hospital. She held no reservations about her interest in Dr. Sam, flirting openly with him whether at work or at social engagements, not caring whether Marilyn was present or not.

Susan had a modelesque figure, not tall but standing five-feet five inches and weighing in at a slender 112 pounds. She had an oval face, beautiful clear skin, and a well proportioned nose and mouth. Below her naturally arched brows her big brown eyes reached out to Dr. Sam from across rooms or amid crowded elevators, following his every move. He could feel it, and he wanted her.

Sometimes in the evening, after eating a quick dinner with his wife and son, Sam made an excuse to leave home. He barely thought of them as the door closed behind him and he sped down the road to meet his new mistress. He drove through the peaceful streets of Bay Village, the evening ripe with possibilities, and thought of Susan's lips, so perfectly shaped and kissable. He imagined the feel of her, so smooth and inviting, of gazing into her eyes and hearing his whispers as their breathing deepened in tandem. Most of all he liked the attention, her feminine hands on him, on his chest, his abs, his manhood. He felt powerful when a woman so attractive desired him.

He drove on, anticipating their encounter. They had great sex, simply no comparison with his wife. He wished he didn't feel that way, but he couldn't stop the passion building up inside him for this new exciting woman. Her confidence attracted him, and he fantasized about her while making his rounds at the hospital and on breaks between patients. He'd lost all desire for Marilyn but still depended on her for his meals, taking care of Chip, cleaning the house, and running errands.

The affair lasted for three years, even after Susan became engaged to another doctor. Eventually Susan moved to California, to Marilyn's great relief, but even then Sam sometimes found excuses to fly out of town.

# # #

On the evening of July 3, 1954, Marilyn busied herself in the kitchen preparing a beautiful dinner. Their neighbors, Nancy and Don Ahern, had already arrived and were sipping cocktails out on the deck with Dr. Sam. Marilyn joined them and all eyes gravitated toward the lake, where fireworks exploded intermittently over the water like brilliant-colored blossoms, a reminder that the Fourth of July was only hours away.

Chip cheerfully played with the Ahern kids, who stayed until after dinner. Then their parents walked them home and tucked them into bed before returning to watch a late-night movie called *Strange Holiday*. The couple settled in on the Sheppard's two-toned, diamond-patterned couch, sitting opposite the window and a couple low-backed armchairs with ruffled skirts.

Sam adjusted the knob on the TV, tweaking the lines on the black and white screen while Marilyn took Chip up to bed. Then she cozied in on Sam's lap in one of the armchairs to watch the movie. He tried to stay awake but found himself dozing off. Before long, he moved over to the daybed just off the living room and fell asleep in his clothes.

When the Aherns left around midnight, Dr. Sam was still sleeping. Marilyn turned off the TV and climbed the stairs to the guest room, where she pulled down the shades, leaving the left one raised a few inches for air.

Behind her, the twin beds stood side-by-side, their headboards against the wall by the door, a nightstand between them. Marilyn removed her clothes and draped them over a rocking chair in the corner. After pulling on her checkered pajamas, she turned down the light and climbed into bed for the very last time.

Darkness settled in around her, and the sheer curtains—hanging in arcs on either side of the double windows—stirred ever-so-slightly in answer to a comforting breeze. Out on Lake Erie, pockets of mist hovered over the water, and the Bay Village neighborhood eased into the calm-hush of night. But a nightmare would soon change all that.

# # #

Suddenly, the most horrible, excruciating pain shot through Marilyn's head, stunning her, disorienting her. Before she could process the why of it, another searing blow slammed into her forehead.

Someone's trying to kill me!

Horrified, she tried to roll away, tried to recognize the figure loaming over her in the dark.

Oh, God no!

Another blow.

Why?

She threw up her hands to block the blows, but another one snapped her finger, cut through skin, crashed into cheekbone and eye socket. The next one nailed her skull, fracturing it like a rare goblet.

Warm blood poured from her head and ran down her face into her eyes, stinging them and blinding her. She felt it pooling beneath her on the bed, could smell it, even taste it, as a frenzy of pain and fear enveloped her.

The feeling of being trapped, never to be free again, weighed heavy as a mountain. She kicked and flailed, and a wave of confusion flooded in. She could hear someone screaming. A woman. Blood curdling screams.

Then she realized it was her.

The blows kept coming—fast, accurate, and deadly.

She felt herself losing strength. The killer grabbed her by the legs and pulled her down violently toward the foot of the bed—pulling her pajama bottoms half down in the process, sliding her top up, exposing her breasts.

I'm dying. . . The reality was unmistakable, and so horribly final.

Chip's sweet little face flashed through her mind.

My son. . . my son. . .

The blows kept coming, but she could no longer feel them. The killer kept swinging over and over and over—even after she quit moving—such was the level of anger and hate.

# # #

At 5:40 a.m., the phone rang like a fire alarm in the Houk's residence. Spencer Houk, mayor of Bay Village, answered with a worried, "Hello," more a question than a greeting. Right away, a very excited Dr. Sheppard blurted into his ear, something about Marilyn being killed. *Killed? Whatever did he mean?* He needed Spencer to come over right away.

Houk, the Mayor of Bay Village, lived a couple houses down. He and his wife, Esther, snapped themselves awake and rushed over to their neighbor's house, aware that something terrible had happened.

They found Dr. Sheppard in his den, reclining in a red chair, without a shirt on. He was cupping the back of his neck in his hands and groaning in pain. Houk sidestepped some sports trophies that had been thrown on the floor, so he could get to Sam's side.

Esther wasted no time going to check on Marilyn. *Surely the doctor had been mistaken*, she thought, trying to reassure herself as she scanned the uncharacteristic disarray in the living room. The desk drawers were open, and crumpled papers, a book, and some trinkets were scattered on the wood floor. *Marilyn couldn't be dead. That just didn't make any sense.*

Esther climbed the stairs in quick succession at first and then slower as she reached the landing. Suddenly she got the urge to turn and run back down, but she steeled herself. She had to check on her neighbor, had to do what she could for her.

Nothing could have prepared Esther for what she saw next. Instead of seeing her pretty, vivacious neighbor lying in a soft, warm bed, she saw a bloodbath surrounding a rumpled body—someone who's bloody, pulverized face she didn't recognize. The dead woman's arms lay limp at her sides and the slender legs were draped over the end of the bed, under the rounded rail of the footboard, an awkward position in any scenario.

Esther stifled a scream and ran back downstairs yelling for her husband to call someone, anyone, for help. After relaying the shocking news, Esther found her way to the whiskey cabinet and poured a shot for Sam, who refused to drink. Not one to imbibe first thing in the morning, Esther didn't hesitate to down the drink herself. This was bad, real bad, and life would never be the same.

Spencer rang the police and did what he could to comfort Dr. Sheppard. Before long, law enforcement, curious neighbors and reporters converged on the scene, turning a once safe and pleasant neighborhood upside down.

Chapter 3: The Investigation

Fred Drenkhan, the first police officer to arrive on scene, answered the call at 5:57 a.m. Five minutes later he was walking through the Sheppard's living room. He noticed a black medical bag upended on the floor, its contents spilling out, as if someone had either dropped the bag in haste or rifled through it. Strange, he thought, as he turned his attention briefly to Dr. Sheppard before making his way upstairs to the victim. She was dead, no question about it.

Bay Village Police would need help, Drenkkan knew this immediately. He summoned Cleveland's Scientific Investigation Unit, and before long, detectives Patrick Gareau and Robert Schottke arrived. By 8:00 a.m. Cuyahoga County Coroner Dr. Sam Gerber marched through the door, believing right away that Dr. Sam did the deed.

Other calls were made, the ones to family being the most difficult. As soon as Dr. Steve arrived, he took charge, insisting upon driving Dr. Sam to Bay View Hospital for an examination. The right side of Sam's face looked swollen, and his neck injury was cause for concern. The third brother, Dr. Richard, carried Chip out to his car and drove him away from the madness.

Dr. Sheppard's quick departure frustrated the detectives, who had wanted to question him further. Sam's telling of events had been murky at best. He claimed that he woke to the sound of his wife screaming, perhaps even calling his name, he didn't know for sure. He stumbled up the stairs to her bedroom only to be confronted by an intruder, maybe two, and a blow to the back of the neck that knocked him out cold.

Sam went on, saying that when he came to, he heard someone knocking about downstairs. Thinking nothing could be done for Marilyn, he ran downstairs and chased the intruder—a tall, bushy-haired man—outside and down a long, steep flight of stairs to the beach where, once again, the assailant assaulted him and knocked him unconscious. When he came to, his shirt was missing and he found himself facedown in the sand, partway in the lake.

The detectives didn't believe him.

Neither did the editors of Cleveland's three daily papers. Journalists, having gotten wind of the unlikely homicide, wasted no time interviewing anyone who could give them a scoop. Thanks to the afternoon headlines, news of the holiday murder spread like a flash flood through the streets of Cleveland and beyond.

# # #

The public needed a guide, such as a lighthouse along shore, to help them navigate the depth of depravity one must have to kill a mother in such a horrible way. The detectives, too, would have to feel their way through the fog. But Dr. Gerber, sure that he knew which way to go, drove to the hospital the day of the murder to interrogate Dr. Sheppard, while the suspect lay in bed with a braced neck and a swollen eye. The beleaguered patient gave the same answers he'd given earlier, refusing to confess despite Gerber's insistence he do so.

From day one, Sheppard couldn't escape the scrutiny. Detectives interrogated him in the hospital on July 8 and again at the Sherriff's office on the 10th with the same results. Not to be stymied, they hit him with accusations of infidelity, specifically about Susan Hayes, asking if he'd had an affair with her. Sam knew this was coming and kept his cool, saying he and she had only been friends.

Again, the detectives didn't believe him. But they would bide their time.

# # #

On July 7, Marilyn was laid to rest in a bronze casket, after a ceremony at Saxton Funeral Home. Her widowed husband sat among the mourners wearing dark glasses and a neck brace—seemingly grieving along with everyone else.

The coroner had removed Marilyn's body from the crime scene the day of the murder but not before neighbors, even a few teenaged boys, had tramped through the house to peek in the murder room and gawk at her beaten, half-naked corpse. No one had secured the crime scene, and it became evident that someone needed to take charge.

But who? Antagonism had developed between the different law enforcement agencies. Bay Village police had their foot in the door, along with Cleveland's police. Both the county sheriff and prosecutor also had a vested interest in the case, as did the coroner, Dr. Gerber.

Gerber, a short, bespeckled man, had both a law degree and a medical degree and had been coroner for nineteen years. The Sheppard case ignited a public outcry, so he wanted to quell the growing unrest and protect his reputation in the process. Soon, he was monopolizing the investigation and doing his part to sway public opinion in the direction of Dr. Sheppard's guilt. In spite of the many police and detectives who wanted in on the action, Dr. Gerber, in his elected position, held the most power. He rubbed some people the wrong way and came off as a know-it-all, but he had his supporters.

One of them was Mary Cowen, who headed the Coroner's Trace Evidence Department. As soon as evidence had been collected from the crime scene, she slipped a white lab coat on over her well-tailored dress and got to work. Walking briskly into the laboratory, she prepared to study the small packets of evidence collected during Marilyn's autopsy. Cowan picked up the first slide and placed it under a microscope on the specimen stage.

She held her breath, trying not to move as she peered through the eyepiece and studied Marilyn's magnified nail clippings. *Interesting*, she thought. *What have we here?* She adjusted the lens, getting a closer look, making note of tiny reddish fibers, possibly from the killer's clothes.

She needed to analyze blood from the crime scene as well, some of which she had collected herself. She typed some blood found in the murder room, which had soaked into the mattress and spattered onto the closet doors. She also tested blood found on a wristwatch belonging to Dr. Sam and another belonging to Marilyn.

Also analyzed was a large spot of blood on Dr. Sam's pants; Cowan compared it to that of Marilyn's, certain it came from either the victim or the killer. She found some of the blood to be similar to both Marilyn's and Sam's, but some of the blood from the crime scene was inconclusive. Dr. Gerber wouldn't like that. Due to some unsatisfying outcomes, she stopped short of analyzing drops from a blood trail that led through the Sheppard's house, thinking the amount inadequate to provide definitive results.

Dr. Adelson, who performed Marilyn's autopsy, estimated her time of death to be between 4:15-4:45 a.m. Nevertheless, Dr. Gerber went on record saying she died earlier, shortly after 3:00 a.m., which didn't bode well for Dr. Sam Sheppard, who failed to call for help until 5:40 a.m.

With each passing day a growing cloud of suspicion fell on Dr. Sheppard, and the media launched a campaign to see him arrested for his wife's murder. They would stop at nothing, as a rash of biting headlines proved. When an arrest didn't materialize immediately, editors started taking aim at Dr. Gerber, criticizing him and forcing his hand.

By now, Sam had sought the advice of an attorney named Bill Corrigan. Sam's counsel advised him not to take a lie detector test, which the media jumped on like a cat on a mouse, one more reason to assume his guilt. Then rumors of the doctor's infidelity shot like a rocket through the streets of Cleveland, and Corrigan advised his client to deny the allegations at all cost.

Reporters went crazy, focusing more on the scandal-mongering aspects of Dr. Sam's private life than anything else, and newspapers flew off the stands.

Then came the inquisition.

Corner Gerber, trying to allay public scrutiny, scheduled an inquest to be held on July 22 at a school gymnasium, where he planned to interrogate Dr. Sam Sheppard most rigorously.

The roomy gymnasium could hold about two hundred spectators, and Gerber saw to it that reporters had the best seats in the house, hopefully guaranteeing his reelection. The morning of the inquest, curiosity seekers began pouring into the gym until the room filled to capacity.

A swarm of media sharks was circling, hungering for Dr. Sheppard's hide, and Dr. Gerber didn't plan to disappoint. He intended to parade the alleged killer in front of the waiting crowd, have him frisked in a dramatic way and then feed him and his sordid secrets to the audience one bloody bite at a time.

Dr. Sam walked into the gym wearing an expensive dark suit, a hard neck brace and, in rather poor taste, a pair of aviator sunglasses that gave him of a shady aura, as if he didn't want to look anyone in the eye. He resented every minute of the proceedings as he sat in front of his interrogator, the reporters, the flashbulbs, the public, and his family. His sunglasses could only do so much to shut out the onslaught, so he rested his right elbow on the table and positioned his hand over his eye, partially concealing his face. At first he looked down as if the glare of the flashbulbs was too bright and the weight of the audience too invasive. Later, he sat back, collapsed his hands in his lap, and crossed his legs jock-style, with ankle resting on knee, determined to defend himself to the bitter end.

Gerber questioned Dr. Sam extensively about the murder itself, and then came the morsel that most fed the tabloids. He asked Sam if he'd had an affair with Susan Hayes, to which Dr. Sam offered a lame denial. Gerber pressed on, asking explicitly if Sam had ever spent the night with her, had ever had sex with her. Again, Sam denied the allegations.

The seven-year itch may have been Dr. Sam's biggest weakness, but denying the Hayes affair would prove to be his biggest downfall.

The inquest dragged on for three days and provided Dr. Gerber a platform from which to repair his battered image and to openly name Dr. Sam as the killer. Gerber's premature and unfair verdict, based more on the suspect's character deficiencies than any hard evidence, began to turn the last of the public against Dr. Samuel Sheppard. All this before he even had his day in court.

# # #

Susan Hayes didn't normally shy away from attention, but flying from California, where she now lived, back to Ohio to be grilled in the wake of a murder, concerning her affair with Dr. Sam, filled her with consternation. As the plane descended she peered out the bubble window at the mob of people below.

A group of determined detectives waited front and center, ready to whisk Ms. Hayes away to a hotel and then to the sheriff's office for questioning. By now the anticipation of the crowd had reached a palpable level, the atmosphere rivaling that of a celebrity's arrival.

Finally Ms. Hayes stepped from the door of the plane, immediately surrounded by authorities, all men, and descended the steps to the tarmac.

She wore her bobbed, light-brown hair brushed back off her face, held a handbag and carry-on bag and wore an unbuttoned sweater over a white floral-print dress. She walked silently with the band of officers and ducked quickly into an unmarked squad car, leaving the crowd chattering behind her.

Over the course of the next few days, the detectives plied some juicy details out of Miss Hayes. These new revelations, coupled with the evidence they already had, convinced them that they had probable cause to make an arrest. They were confident that a Grand Jury would indict Dr. Sheppard for first-degree murder.

Preparing mentally for his impending arrest, the doctor retreated to his parent's house, where he waited for the legal ax to fall and chop away at what was left of his life.

Chapter 4: The Trial of the Century

Twenty-six days after Marilyn's murder, a Cuyahoga County deputy arrested Dr. Sam. The officer cuffed his own wrist to the doctor's and covered their joined hands with a coat, as if that would fool anyone. The media ate it up.

Sam braced himself for the murder trial, which kicked into gear on the eighteenth of October. Flashbulbs exploded in his face as deputies led him from the jailhouse to the courthouse. In the courtroom, upwards of sixty reporters clamored for dibs on a limited number of seats.

The jury would have a choice of verdicts; they could find Dr. Samuel Sheppard innocent or guilty, with guilty verdicts ranging from manslaughter on up to first-degree murder; the latter of which could carry the death penalty depending on the mercy of the jury.

The seventy-year old Judge, Edward Blythn, was convinced that the man on trial had murdered his pregnant wife, and he voiced his opinion to various individuals, setting a perilous tone for the trial in question. Feeling as he did, he refused to move the proceedings to a different county in spite of the explosive media coverage.

On the third of November, jury selection was complete, and prosecutors immediately made arrangements to transport the jury members to the murder scene. The panel of twelve filed onto a city bus for the trip to Lake Erie, half curious, half apprehensive at the thought of walking into the house where someone had bludgeoned a pregnant mother to death.

As the bus rumbled toward the house on Lake Road, jurors looked out the fogged-up windows, astonished at the number of people crowding the property in hopes of stealing a glimpse of the man on trial.

Dr. Sheppard sat with hands cuffed in the back of a cruiser. He felt a pit in the bottom of his stomach as the officer steered into the driveway of his once beautiful home. Now he would enter as a prisoner, no longer allowed to ask intrusive strangers to stay out and get off his property. *Horrible.* To top it off, he would be handcuffed to a deputy like a dog on a leash as he walked through the life he once lived.

The silent entourage trudged through the snow-encrusted yard with their heads down and entered the cold house. The men and women, most dressed in long winter coats and somber expressions, shuffled from room to room, the women clutching their purses, the men stuffing their clammy hands in their pockets.

Sam and the deputy, looking like Siamese twins, pulled up the rear and left the gaggle of onlookers behind to crane their necks and wait. Overhead, a deafening helicopter hovered, giving its occupants a bird's-eye view.

Sam wanted to close his eyes and make the nightmare disappear. He clung to the hope that the jury would find him innocent, that he could return to his work at the hospital, retrieve his son, put his life back together and put this all behind him. He let his eyes wander through the house, and at the sight of his son's bedroom he couldn't hold back. It didn't matter who could hear him, the tears poured down his cheeks, and his half-muffled sobs echoed through the home.

Back at the courthouse, Corrigan couldn't believe that Judge Blythin had allowed reporters to snap pictures of the jury. As expected, someone leaked the names and photos to the press, and they were published for all the world to see. Corrigan was outraged, but the judge shot his objections down, and the trial proceeded.

John Mahon, the assistant county prosecutor, stood before the jury and gave his opening statement. The jury listened attentively while he pontificated on Dr. Sheppard's version of events, with just the right amount of derision. Dr. Sam had to come up with a story, Mahon suggested, to explain why he had been down on the beach after the murder, why he had gotten wet, why his t-shirt was missing, why his keychain and bloody watch had been removed—only to be found tossed in the bushes in a bag that belonged to him. None of it, Mahon emphasized, made sense. The defendant had staged a robbery to divert attention from the real crime, a domestic homicide.

Mahon went on to talk about motive, stating that Dr. Sheppard's womanizing and most recent affair were the motivation. The couple, he insisted, must have fought over Sam's philandering, leaving Marilyn beaten to death. Dr. Sam's injuries, pale in comparison, could easily have been self-inflicted. The jury sat stone-faced, weighing the evidence, studying the defendant, thinking about the victim.

Fred Garmone opened for the defense and zeroed in on the authority's rush to judgment, which had resulted in a paltry investigation. Sam and Marilyn had been getting along, were excited about the pregnancy. He had no reason to kill her.

The state's first witness, coroner Lester Adelson, displayed huge slides of Marilyn's face and head from her autopsy, close-ups of her horrific wounds that elicited a chorus of gasps from the jurors and spectators alike. He saved her skinless, hairless skull for the grand finale, a move that would lead future appeals courts to rule such images prejudicial. Dr. Sheppard bowed his head in his hands and fought back tears, unable to look at the grisly images of his wife but forced to listen to the descriptions nonetheless.

More evidence followed. Before her death, Marilyn had disclosed personal details to Nancy Ahern, who stepped up to the witness stand resigned to be honest even if it didn't flatter Dr. Sheppard. Assistant prosecutor, Thomas Parrino, questioned her regarding the defendant, wondering if she had ever heard, even secondhand, that he had discussed divorce. Nancy's answer in the affirmative amounted to hearsay, but Judge Blythin allowed it in anyway.

All during the trial, reporters raced in and out of the courtroom to phone in the latest breaking news, and Judge Blythn pounded his gavel repeatedly to staunch one outburst after another, overruling many of Corrigan's vehement objections.

When Dr. Gerber took the stand, assistant prosecutor Saul Danaceau took the floor, letting the coroner describe what he had seen the morning of the murder and how he had helped remove the victim's body from the bloodstained bed. Gerber's testimony about the murder weapon, which had never been recovered, was a blow to the defense. He claimed it had been a surgical instrument, an opinion based on an apparent imprint on Marilyn's pillow that no one could explain. But even Dr. Gerber couldn't pinpoint what kind of surgical instrument it might have been. It could have just as easily been a flashlight, a fireplace poker, or a bedside lamp.

During cross-examination Corrigan countered the prosecution's claim that no fingerprints could be found at the crime scene. The prosecution wanted to promote the idea that the killer had wiped away all prints, when in actuality, prints were present but simply unidentifiable.

The state saved their most intriguing witness, Susan Hayes, for last. They wanted her testimony to be fresh in the jurors' minds before the defense took the floor.

Earlier, Susan had entered the courthouse wearing a mink coat. Now she walked into the courtroom looking elegant even in a prim black dress that covered everything from the base of her neck on down to her knees. She wore her light brown hair short, curled, and capped with a black velvet bow hat.

The jury heard all the sordid details, how the doctor had given her presents—an expensive coat, a ring, a watch—how they'd had sex in his car, in the interns' apartment, and how, four months before the murder, Susan had accompanied her married lover to a party in California at the home of some friends. No, he had never promised her marriage. She left the stand not looking at Sam.

Corrigan and Garmone joined forces, calling the Sheppard brothers to testify right out of the gate—first Dr. Steve, then Dr. Richard. Though the brothers did their best to downplay their brother's extramarital affairs and the seriousness of the Sheppard's marital problems, at the end of the day, their testimony made little difference to the jury.

Everyone wondered if the famous defendant would take the stand in his own defense. Dr. Sam wanted to testify; after all, his character had been assassinated by the media for months. Here was an opportunity to give his version of events, to show the jury who he really was and to hopefully convince them that he was a respectable guy who couldn't have killed his wife just because he cheated on her.

Sam had the final say and chose to testify. He described how he woke up to hear Marilyn screaming for help, calling for him, and how he scrambled up the stairs half awake only to be presented with the horror of his wife being beaten. He saw the outline of the killer standing before him in the darkened room, hazy as if in a dream. He repeated how he would later struggle with this same man after chasing him out of the house and down fifty-two stairs to the beach. His story didn't waver.

After all the witnesses had testified, Parrino hit a homerun with his portion of the closing arguments, appealing to the jurors to use commonsense in debating the plausibility of the defendant's version of events. He questioned Dr. Sam's whereabouts during the murder, how swinging that many brutal blows took time. He reminded the jury that Dr. Samuel Sheppard stood over six feet tall, weighing in at 180 pounds. How could he, a star athlete, have been so easily subdued during a life and death struggle?

Sal Danaceau, in his portion of the closing arguments, honed in on why it took Sam so long to call for help; plenty of time had elapsed after his wife's murder, giving Dr. Sheppard a chance to get rid of his shirt and the murder weapon, and to stage a burglary.

Testimony dragged on for forty-three days, culminating at the height of the holiday season. The jury slipped away for deliberations on December 17th. As snow swept across Cleveland, Dr. Sam huddled in his jail cell, nervously awaiting the verdict. The jurors reappeared five days later with a verdict in hand, just in time for Christmas.

Dr. Sheppard stood on rubbery legs, trying to look calm while awaiting the verdict, but the suspense rattled him. At any moment he would hear his fate as decided by the jury, twelve strangers who stood in judgment of him, a man none of them knew beyond the media coverage and trial proceedings. He would either spring to freedom just in time to share Christmas with his son or be led back to his cell to await prison, maybe even the death penalty.

At the turn of two phrases, Dr. Sam went from momentary elation—at hearing he'd been found innocent of first-degree murder—only to be broadsided with a second-degree murder conviction. He would face life in prison, one of the worse outcomes he could have hoped for. That he'd be eligible for parole in ten years was little comfort. He walked back to his cell in turmoil, anger and sadness swirling around inside him like a hot blizzard. He was ruined, his life was all but over, but he would fight it. He would appeal his verdict and find a way to win like he always had before.

Chapter 5: Prison Life

Instead of going to prison right away, Dr. Sam remained in county jail while awaiting appeal. The verdict hadn't even sunk in yet when his brother, Steve, dropped another bomb. Their mother, Ethel Sheppard, distraught over Sam's conviction, shot herself in the head on January 7, 1955. The news devastated Sam.

Perhaps out of pity, Dr. Sheppard's jailers deemed him furlough eligible and allowed him to attend her funeral, but he was cuffed to the arm of a deputy throughout the service. He curled up on his bunk that night and fought back tears, wondering if things could get any worse. They could.

On January 18, little more than a week later, Sam received some more bad news. His father had passed away as well, finally succumbing to stomach cancer. Sam didn't know how much more he could take. He could still feel his father's hand on his, could still hear his warm voice encouraging him to keep forging ahead, to keep hoping for that one day when truth would prevail.

# # #

His father's death made him think of Chip. Writing to his son had become a constant, one of the only ways he could reach out to the lost and grieving boy, but the prison system didn't provide for a very nurturing atmosphere for father and son bonding. Whatever Christmas or birthday presents he could send to his son seemed trivial in such a time of loss and mourning.

Sam needed a thread of hope to hang on to, and Bill Corrigan provided one. Bill had contacted a leading criminalist named Dr. Paul Kirk out of California, who agreed to help with the case. It took Kirk three months to sift through the files and write up a report, and his insights were a boon to the defense.

After Kirk's very detailed, scientific investigation, he came to the conclusion that a third person must have been in the Sheppard home that night. And based on the evidence, Kirk dismissed Gerber's claim that the murder weapon was a surgical instrument. A heavy flashlight, he deduced, had caused Marilyn's injuries and was likely carried into the house by an intruder.

The criminalist also performed a thorough analysis of the blood evidence, finding spots that very well could have belonged to someone other than the victim or her husband. Armed with Dr. Kirk's 19-page report, Corrigan filed a motion for a new trial. Three months later the court of appeals denied it.

Devastated by the setback, Dr. Sheppard asked to be transferred to prison. A whole year had passed since his wife's murder, and Sam had been cooped up in county jail without any fresh air or exercise. The state prison turned out to be an intimidating, bleak facility in Columbus, Ohio, but at least Sam could spend his days outside in the prison yard while Corrigan continued to fight for his freedom.

The newly transferred prisoner worked to win the friendship and respect of his fellow inmates. Size and strength could be a good thing in the joint, and his reputation preceded him, but the other prisoners still expected him to prove himself. To Sam's relief they didn't take the media's word for much of anything. If the doctor treated them squarely, showed them respect and kept his nose out of their business, he'd be accepted and given respect in return. It didn't hurt that he had money either.

Behind bars, the outside world faded away, and prison took on a life of its own. Dr. Sam busied himself tutoring other inmates and joining the prison's wrestling team, rising to the top like he'd done years ago in school. Soon he graduated to office duties and then was promoted to the prison medical ward. It couldn't compare to working at Bay Village Hospital, but at least he could put his skills to work helping prisoners who'd fallen ill or suffered injuries. As a free man, Dr. Sam had handled many emergencies; now he could assist the prison doctors who treated some of the more common prison traumas—the aftermath of suicides, rapes and knifings.

In the fall of 1969, a name from the past caught the attention of law enforcement officers. Richard Eberling, who had once washed the Sheppard's windows, was arrested for larceny, having in his possession some rings that used to belong to Marilyn Sheppard, rings that he'd stolen from her in-law's house after her death.

Eberling had been questioned during the initial murder investigation, as had anyone else who'd been in the Sheppard home, but no one found him of much interest. Now he raised some suspicion. While questioning him, the cops were taken aback when Eberling admitted, without much provocation, that he had bled in the Sheppard's home a couple days before Marilyn's murder. He said he nicked his hand while washing the kitchen window and dripped blood from room to room. In spite of this admission and the implications it held, Eberling, after spending a short stint in jail, was let go and more or less forgotten. At least for a while.

# # #

The years dragged by, and Dr. Sheppard's old life—the one where he performed surgery and felt respected and in control—faded with the seasons. The Fourth of July always came down hard.

July hadn't been a good month for Marilyn, and it didn't turn out to be a good month for Bill Corrigan either. He died at the end of July, seven years after Marilyn but by less dubious means.

F. Lee Bailey, a dark-haired, cigar-smoking, hungry young attorney, filled the void. Fairly convinced of Sam's innocence, he ignited a public relations campaign meant to rebrand Dr. Sheppard in the public eye to pave the way for his release from prison. Bailey also appealed to the governor and anyone else who could pull strings. This forward-thinking young attorney believed that if he could work the media angle and even appear on TV, he could turn things around.

The Sheppard case no longer permeated the news quite as much nor dominated the conversations in restaurants and cocktail lounges—or in the cars that rolled slowly past the eerie murder house along the lake.

And then came Ariane.

Dr. Sam corresponded with a number of people, one of whom was a woman named Ariane Tebbenjohanns. She was of German descent and initiated the contact. Dr. Sheppard, who had an eye for a pretty lady and a heart lonely for love, responded enthusiastically. They embarked on a letter-writing whirlwind that eventually led to a romantic relationship. It added a spark to his mundane existence, especially when she sent pretty pictures of herself and supported him through his appeals.

Ariane was an adventure seeking blond, glamorous and dripping with money, some of which she donated to Sam's cause. In 1963, she flew to America in the middle of winter to meet this man whom she'd been flirting with from across the Atlantic and falling for through letters. It flattered her that he found her attractive, and what could give a woman the feeling of importance more than a man who was starving for female companionship? He told her things that he'd never told his long-dead wife, telling her that he'd never known such love could exist.

The media got wind of the impending visit and converged on the airport while her plane was in flight, every reporter wanting to be the first to break the story about this wealthy German jetsetter. She strutted across the tarmac in a leopard print coat, surrounded by a herd of men. Her platinum, bouffant hair stood out along with the white pearly balls dangling from her ears and her big white-toothed smile. She wore heavy black eyeliner and dressed in the latest fashions, exuding confidence and sex appeal. Hooking up with Dr. Sam had thrust her into the national spotlight, bringing with it excitement, publicity and fame. She was no shrinking violet and the camera loved her as much as she loved it.

The night before Ariane's visit Dr. Sheppard could barely sleep, and morning couldn't come fast enough. His heart raced wildly as he walked into the visiting room, and when he saw her in the flesh for the first time he felt like the luckiest man in the world. He couldn't believe his good fortune. Her beauty and presence surpassed his expectations, and the chemistry between them lit up the dreary visiting center. The authorities allowed them to kiss hello, a kiss that they both cherished. Then they sat and talked, smiling the whole while.

Dr. Sheppard had become accustomed to a colorless world, one of muted grey tones made up of stone and steel. Gazing upon Ariane lit up his senses, her bright blond hair, her red lipstick, her porcelain skin, and the vibrant color of her clothes.

They spoke of marriage and dreamed of the day when they might be together. The fantasy sustained them when they were apart, never occurring to them that it would be impossible to live up to in the real world.

Ariane made arrangements to stay in Ohio, hoping that Sam might be released soon. Used to being stared at everywhere she went, she became a media magnet, unintentionally drawing attention away from and sabotaging efforts to free her famous fiancé from prison. What Ariane wanted, she got. And when the prison suspended her visiting and writing privileges due to the hoopla, she sent a love letter to Sam via the *Dispatch*, one of Cleveland's dailies, which was all too happy to oblige her and published the open love letter to her fiancé.

# # #

Early in 1963, the parole board held a meeting, and Sam was banking on being let out. His attorney, however, wanted Sam's conviction overturned, so when parole was denied, Bailey filed a petition of habeas corpus in Ohio's federal district court. With a trio of law school students onboard, he put together a plethora of evidence, which he presented to Judge Weinman, detailing how Sheppard's rights had been violated. The judge listened with an open mind.

Finally, on July 15, 1964, Bailey succeeded in getting Dr. Sheppard released from prison. But much work lay ahead. The state of Ohio would waste no time appealing the Judge's decision. Dr. Sheppard didn't let that fact dampen his excitement as he walked out of prison for the first time in ten years. Baily picked him up at the gate and drove him straight to a hotel to hook up with Ariane. Sam couldn't wait to take her in his arms; soon they would lie together—man and woman, husband and wife.

A caravan of reporters followed them to the hotel and planned to trail them, certain that wedding bells would ring. Their suspicions proved correct. Dr. Sheppard and Ariane wasted no time going to the Cook County Clerk's office to obtain a marriage license. She wore an elegantly hooded, zebra-print dress with no sleeves and long white gloves. She looked up at him adoringly as he held their license and their future in his hands. No, they hadn't spent any sensible time together on the outside, but they couldn't wait.

An entourage consisting of Dr. Sam, Ariane, Bailey and his wife, and a newspaper man named Paul Holmes dodged paparazzi and dashed to Chicago to hold a quickie wedding in a hotel suite. Holmes rode along, promising the couple they could stay in the honeymoon suite compliments of the *Chicago Tribune* in exchange for an exclusive.

A tall slender man, Magistrate Nickolas Kure, performed the ceremony. Sam and Ariane stood before him while reciting their vows, their expressions loving but serious. Sam held Ariane's hand as if it was a rare and fragile flower and gazed down at her. She wore a black dress with a black lacey bodice and her favorite dangly earrings. She had her shiny blond hair puffed up on top of her head and tied in the back with a large bow at the base of her neck. At last, after their passionate prison courtship, they shared their first kiss as man and wife.

Four days later, after a short honeymoon in New York, the newly married Dr. Sheppard picked up his second wife, fur coat and all, and carried her across the threshold of their new home in Rocky River, Ohio. Excitement and well-wishes filled the air around them and their tightknit group of supporters.

At the end of summer, Bailey filed a writ with the Supreme Court. He ruminated on the poor investigation, the previous judge's bias, and the media's vindictive and unending attacks against the prime suspect. It worked. In November, the court decided Bailey could appear before the Supreme Court and present his oral argument. Such an opportunity didn't come along very often.

Dr. Sheppard drove Ariane's white coupe out of their garage and parked it in the driveway. Today his new wife would accompany him to Washington for his upcoming hearing. For the drive, he dressed in brown slacks and a casual waist-length jacket over a white shirt and tie. He smiled broadly as he opened the passenger door for his wife. She was draped in a black mink coat with a white shawl collar and matching sleeve cuffs. Her trademark earrings—pearly ball swinging on gold-tone chain—dangled from each ear. She looked like one of James Bond's girls.

Joy bubbled over, filling the air wherever they went, so happy were they in the honeymoon phase of their marriage. If people didn't know any better, they would never have guessed that these two were heading to a murder hearing.

The Supreme Court justices, in a landmark court decision, overturned Dr. Sheppard's murder conviction on constitution grounds. He could enjoy his freedom for now but could face another trial down the road. Still, the ruling was a huge victory for the defense.

While the newlyweds relished their first few months together, the prosecuting attorney announced that a retrial was imminent. Dr. Sheppard didn't want to dwell on the bad news, but he packed a bag of clothes and kept it by the bed in the event of another arrest. With the threat of a second trial hanging over his head, his mood jumped up and down like a pogo stick. To cope with the anxiety, he popped pills and drank heavily, usually vodka, which was Ariane's drink of choice. She often had a drink in one hand and a cigarette in the other. A couple months into their marriage, she started experiencing little waves of nausea and made an appointment to see a doctor. After a checkup, her suspicions were confirmed: she was pregnant.

A year later, she and Sam celebrated their first wedding anniversary, spending the day enjoying the sun and swimming in an outdoor pool. Sam, dripping wet, wrapped his arms around his wife, who sat at the edge of the pool and had yet to get in the water. They looked great together, like models in a swimwear ad, as they posed for a snapshot to commemorate the occasion. He wore swimming trunks, a gold bracelet and a pinky ring. Ariane looked smashing in a black and white polka dotted bikini, her blond hair and makeup perfectly made up. Neither revealed the pressure they were under as Sam's second trial loomed on the horizon.

Chapter 6: The Second Trial

Dr. Sheppard stood on the steps outside the courthouse with one arm around his eighteen-year old son, Chip (who now went by the name Samuel Jr.) and one arm around Ariane. Moments earlier Dr. Sheppard had stood before a judge and entered a not guilty plea. Samuel Jr. had grown into a handsome young man. He wore black-framed glasses and a smart looking dark suit and tie, his thick light-brown hair parted to the side.

The second trial started on November 1, 1966. As the courthouse proceedings got underway, the sky drizzled outside and the mood sizzled inside. As the testimony dragged on, however, the jurors strained to stay focused on the more mundane aspects of the trial. Gone was the circus atmosphere that had cartwheeled its way through the first trial. The judge, Francis J. Talty, put in place strict courtroom guidelines, refusing to allow any cameras in the courtroom. He also sequestered the jurors. They were let out only to be shuttled to the scene of the crime by way of a city bus. Dr. Sam no longer owned the house but walked through the rooms a stranger.

The prosecution team consisted of John Corrigan and Leo Spellacy. Corrigan shared the same last name as Dr. Sam's original defense attorney but was of no relation. Just as the prosecution had done in the first trial, this team called Coroner Gerber to the stand. He still believed very strongly that Dr. Sheppard had murdered Marilyn and clung to his claim that the murder weapon had been a surgical instrument.

They also called Gerber's colleague Mary Cowan back to the stand to testify about blood analysis, particularly about the spatter on the man's watch found at the murder scene. The prosecution thought this was the smoking gun that would seal another murder conviction. Cowan's testimony confirmed their stance. She claimed that the blood could only have gotten on the watch at the time of the murder, due to the extended shape of the droplets. The watch, she believed, had been worn by Dr. Sheppard while he bludgeoned his wife to death.

When Bailey got a crack at Cowan, however, he pushed her into a corner. He got her to admit that she neither had the knowledge necessary nor the hands-on experience needed to make such claims. The prosecutors started to sweat a little.

During the trial, Bailey steered the focus away from Sam's marital infidelities and employed an alternate-suspect scenario, leading jurors to wonder if, indeed, a third person had been dripping blood from a cut in the home that night.

Neither side called Susan Hayes as a witness this time around. Since the first trial, she'd been married, and the prosecutors felt it unnecessary to drag her back into the muck so many years later.

At the opportune time, Bailey presented Dr. Kirk's findings, which supported the defense's position regarding the watch and blood spatter evidence. He demonstrated how the blood must have dripped onto the watch from an open wound, after the watch had been ripped from Dr. Sheppard's wrist. Since Dr. Sheppard had no open wounds at the time, it must have been the killer's blood, perhaps from a bite wound. Some of Marilyn's upper teeth had been broken during the struggle. She could well have bitten the killer's hand and broken her teeth in the process while fighting for her life.

Dr. Sheppard, who was once again fighting for his life, took Bailey's advice and refrained from taking the stand this time around. It proved to be a good move. The jury found Dr. Samuel Sheppard not guilty.

Chapter 7: Later Life

With the long nightmare finally behind him, Dr. Sheppard tried to put his life back together, but he still wrestled with the stigma of his previous murder conviction. Even so, he hoped to get his surgeons license reinstated so he could get back to the work he loved. It took some time, but he finally succeeded. Nevertheless, the professional success he'd known before prison eluded him. He hadn't been in an operating room for twelve years and had lost his touch. After accidentally cutting the artery of one patient and then another, resulting in the patients' deaths, the medical board revoked his license, and the victims' families sued.

Sam resorted to opening a small medical practice, but despised the mundane routine, thinking the treating of common ailments beneath him. He soon grew bored. Drowning in self-pity, he routinely soused himself with vodka and medicated himself with barbiturates. Ariane would later admit to his exploiting his position as a doctor to acquire drugs illegally for recreational use and to self-medicate.

The marriage soon soured and the couple separated. She complained about him spending too much of her money, and he accused her of being a controlling personality. They divorced in 1969.

Dr. Sheppard didn't let anything beat him, not even losing his second wife to divorce. He became a professional wrestler at the age of forty-five, and this gave him a new lease on life. He had a goal to shoot for again and he liked the challenge of it. Thankfully, wrestling in prison had kept him in excellent shape. He felt proud of his physique and agreed to pose for promotional shots wearing only black shorts and tight-laced black wrestling shoes. He and his wrestling partner and promoter, George Strickland, posed in ready stances with their legs braced and arms up in a show of strength, like they were ready to box or go on a quick defense—a mindset that Dr. Sam had become all too familiar with over the years.

Thinking Sam's presence might draw a bigger crowd, Strickland put out a press release that included a photo of Dr. Sheppard holding a poster advertising the event. Wearing his white doctor's coat with a stethoscope hanging out the front pocket, Sam held up the black and white poster, which provided the names of the participants as well as the place and time. The match, scheduled for Saturday August 9, 1969, would be held at Waverly High School. Farmer Miller and Black Panther would take the mat for the opening match; after which, Wild Bill Scholl and Dr. Sam Sheppard would compete in the semifinals. Strickland and Dr. Wiltberger would go up against The Iron Russians in the main event.

Dr. Sheppard's life had veered off in yet another direction, and over time, the relationship he had with his two brothers fell into disrepair. They distanced themselves from him, unable to help him with his drug and alcohol abuse or the other detrimental choices he made.

To ease his loneliness, Dr. Sheppard took up with Colleen Strickland, the twenty-year old daughter of his wrestling partner. A blond like his second wife, Colleen had a heavier build and lacked the sophistication, but she was younger and possessed a sweeter demeanor. Due to the age difference, they didn't have a lot in common but came back from a trip to Mexico claiming they'd gotten married.

Dr. Sheppard's dependencies on drugs and alcohol plagued him right up until the end. He collapsed and died on April 26, 1970 in the Strickland's home. He was forty-six years old. His body gave out due to liver disease most likely brought on by his alcoholism. Ariane showed up for the funeral, grieving genuinely for the man she had once been married to. Only one of Sam's brothers attended the funeral. The other, Steven, was in London. Sam's son, who was in Spain, didn't make it home for his dad's funeral, but he would go on a legal crusade in the years to come in an effort to clear his father's name.

Chapter 8: Legacy

Before his death, Dr. Sheppard wrote, with the help of a ghostwriter, the story of his legal battle. The book, *Endure and Conquer*, gave him the opportunity to tell his side of the story at last, free from media bias, courtroom restrictions, and opposing points of view.

Numerous other books were written about the Sheppard case as well. Among the authors were family members (such as his brother, Steve Sheppard, and his son, Samuel Reese Sheppard) to legal experts, such as F. Lee Bailey and Paul Holmes. Each new book shed a little more light on the case, on the man, and on the victim and provided photos of the once happy family. But none of books, either by themselves or as a whole, could completely solve the ongoing mystery.

Once Dr. Sheppard was exonerated, no one else was ever thoroughly investigated or charged, which left a hole in the lives of his surviving family members.

Toward the end of Dr. Sheppard's prison term, when public sentiment started shifting in his favor, a new TV Series began to air called *The Fugitive*. Much like Dr. Sheppard's ordeal, this fictional character was a handsome doctor who had been convicted of murdering his wife. Unlike Sheppard, this man escaped on the way to prison and set out to prove his innocence. The dramatic series aired from 1963-1967 before fading into obscurity—Once Dr. Sheppard had been released, the show lost some of its tension and pizzazz. Years later, the script would be resurrected and turned into a major motion picture, and most new viewers would have no idea that a real-to-life case, mirroring the movie, had once permeated the media in the mid-twentieth century and had shattered the lives of a family.

The books and movie helped to immortalize the Sheppard case. But one of the more important outcomes came by way of the Supreme Court ruling in which Dr. Sheppard's murder conviction was overturned. This Landmark case paved the way for fairer trials and would be cited over and over again in future court cases. The murder and its aftermath also became the topic of lectures, prompting many professionals to write speeches about this classic murder mystery. But even after all this, the famous house on the lake continued to hold its secrets.

Conclusion

Like a sunken ship at the bottom of Lake Erie, the truth about Marilyn's murder remained deep in the depths of the past, in a murky environment difficult to navigate. Fragments of the killer's identity could be discovered but not successfully brought to the surface, not in any recognizable form.

The police questioned Richard Eberling on several occasions and gave him a lie detector test, later found to be inconclusive. A jury even convicted him of the murder of another woman and the forgery of her will. But no one ever charged him with Marilyn's murder even though he was as good a suspect as her husband.

Neither the Supreme Court's ruling nor the not guilty verdict could put to rest the speculation surrounding Dr. Sheppard. It followed him for the rest of his life, even hounding him after his death. Whether his fate was justice for a brutal killing or the worst possible luck to befall an innocent man was still a mystery to many.

The Sheppards had a beautiful home and over 30,000 square miles of water in their backyard to enjoy to their hearts' content. But water can both save a life and take a life—and the same could be said about a doctor.

But what of the victim? Who will speak for her and the life she was in the middle of living? Who will listen for her whispers on the breeze, calling her son's name, calling to her unborn baby, calling to whomever will listen the name of her killer. . .who will avenge her murder and find the final piece of the puzzle, waiting to be held up to the light, its mystery forever deep, dark and cold?

Bibliography

Cooper, Cynthia Cooper. Sam Reese Sheppard. *Mockery of Justice*. New York: Penguin Group, 1995.

Evans, Colin. *A Question of Evidence*. New Jersey: John Wiley and Sons, 2003.

Holmes, Paul. Retrial: *Murder and Dr. Sam Sheppard*. New York: Bantam Books, 1966.

Neff, James. *The Wrong Man. The Final Verdict on the Dr. Sam Sheppard Murder Case*. New York: Random House, 2002.

"The Case of Doctor Samuel Sheppard": http://www.trutv.com/library/crime/notorious.

"The Trials of Dr. Sam Sheppard: A Chronology." http://law2.umkc.edu/faculty/projects/ftrials/sheppard/sheppardchonology.html.

Wecht M.D. J.D., Cyril. Greg Saitz. *Mortal Evidence: The Forensics Behind Nine Shocking Cases.* New York: Prometheus, 2003.

Made in United States
Troutdale, OR
05/31/2024

20239803R00066